GREAT
t-SHIRT
GRAPHICS
2

First published in the United States of America by:
Rockport Publishers, Inc.
146 Granite Street
Rockport, Massachusetts 01966
Telephone: (508) 546-9590
Fax: (508) 546-7141

Distributed to the book trade and art trade in the U.S. by:
North Light, an imprint of
F & W Publications
1507 Dana Avenue
Cincinnati, Ohio 45207
Telephone: (513) 531-2222

Other distribution by:
Rockport Publishers, Inc.
Rockport, Massachusetts 01966

ISBN 1-56496-180-X

10 9 8 7 6 5 4 3 2 1

Art Director: Laura P. Herrmann
Cover & Book Design: Supon Design Group
Layout: H. A. Lind
Production Manager: Barbara States
Production Assistant: Pat O'Maley
Cover Photography: (Front cover, from the top far right)
                    Sackett Design
                    Dyer/Mutchnick Group, Inc.
                    Lehner & Whyte
                    Gil Schuler Graphic Design, Inc.
                    High Cotton, Inc.
                    Clifford Selbert Design
                    (Back cover)
                    PandaMonium Designs
Additional Photography: The Finer Image

Printed in Hong Kong

GREAT t-SHIRT GRAPHICS 2

ROCKPORT
PUBLISHERS

Rockport Publishers, Rockport, Massachusetts

Distributed by North Light Books, Cincinnati, Ohio

INTRODUCTION

People of all cultures, nationalities, and ages wear T-shirts. As popular as jeans, T-shirts can be wearable art, or a forum to express political statements, religious beliefs, or preferences running from wild life to wild parties, and everything in between.

The key to the T-shirt's popularity lies in its ability to be whatever you want. Placing an image on fabric can be as simple as tie-dying in your washing machine at home or as complex as creating the full-color, high-tech designs of the Grateful Dead.

This design flexibility is best demonstrated in your local T-shirt shop, where you'll see everything from golf humor and Gary Larson cartoons to reproductions of paintings by Matisse, Dali, and Picasso.

VISITING A T-SHIRT SHOP IS A LITTLE LIKE VISITING AN ART GALLERY, EXCEPT VISITORS CAN TAKE THE ARTWORK HOME.

T-shirt created by Marlene Montgomery Design.

Artists of the past, and even scientific greats such as Einstein, have regained popularity because of the T-shirt. A new design trend has current celebrities—such as jazz trumpeter Miles Davis—showing the world their artwork and paintings printed on T-shirts.

For me, the fascination with T-shirts began when I answered an advertisement for a graphic designer. This lead to assignment after assignment creating images for T-shirts. Since then, there's been no going back. I'm hooked! The creative energy I get whenever I see someone walking around in one of my designs…

"HEY, I'M THE DESIGNER OF THAT T-SHIRT YOUR WEARING, "

I silently shout—has helped me launch a successful business of my own. T-shirts are such an astounding medium, their images are not contained by walls, not limited by galleries or a single canvas. Many people can share in the art experience at once.

T-SHIRTS ARE FOR EVERYONE.

MARLENE MONTGOMERY, OWNER AND OPERATOR OF MARLENE MONTGOMERY DESIGN, CHICAGO, ILLINOIS

Design Firm: Clifford Selbert Design
All Design: Linda Kondo, Stephanie Wade
Photographer: Peter Rice, Joel Levine
Client: Converse, Inc.
Purpose or Occasion: Promotion
Number of Colors: 4
This T-shirt depicts the classic *Converse All Stars* sneakers and was used as a marketing piece.

Design Firm: Spirit River Design
Art Director: Steven Pikala
Designers: Steven Pikala, Michael Hudson
Illustrator: Steven Pikala
Client: Hugh O'Brien Youth Foundation
Purpose or Occasion: Motivational
Number of Colors: 4
This graphic design is intended to inspire participants at a weekend retreat for young people who show leadership abilities.

Design Firm: Morla Design
Art Director: Jennifer Morla
Designers: Jennifer Morla, Sharrie Brooks
Client: Capp Street Project
Purpose or Occasion: Promotion
Number of Colors: 2

Capp Street Project

Capp Street Project

Capp Street Project

▶

Design Firm: Karyl Klopp Design

All Design: Karyl Klopp

Client: JAH SPIRIT

Purpose or Occasion: Promotion for the band

Number of Colors: 4

This shirt design employs a collage of "cut-out" instruments used by the band. The words "JAH SPIRIT" and the band logo were accentuated by using black and white.

◀

Design Firm: Sayles Graphic Design

All Design John Sayles

Client: Allied Life

Purpose or Occasion: Commemoration of a company trip

Number of Colors: 4

A coordinating gift box makes this sweatshirt a nice memento.

Design Firm: Alex Paradowski Graphic Design
Art Director: Alex Paradowski
Designer: Stephen Cox
Illustrator: Stephen Cox
Client: Alex Paradowski Graphic Design
Purpose or Occasion: Company float trip
Number of Colors: 4

▲

Design Firm: Rickabaugh Graphics

All Design: Eric Rickabaugh

Illustrators: Eric Rickabaugh, Tony Meuser

Client: Rickabaugh Graphics/Design Works

Purpose or Occasion: Retail

Number of Colors: 2

Two self-promotional T-shirts created for sale
in the studio's retail outlet, *Design Works*.

◀

Design Firm: PandaMonium Designs

All Design: Raymond Yu

Client: Ka-Boom! Sportswear

Purpose or Occasion: Retail

Number of Colors: 5

A variety of T-shirts designed for retail sale
targeted at the tourism market.

Design Firm: Rickabaugh Graphics

All Design: Mark Krumel

Client: City of Columbus—Recreation & Parks Department

Purpose or Occasion: Jazz & Rib Festival

Number of Colors: 3

The festival logo was broken apart to create some movement and energy. The shirts were sold to raise money for the Recreation and Parks Department and to create awareness.

Design Firm: Gil Shuler Graphic Design, Inc.
All Design: Gil Shuler
Client: Atlantis Coastal Foods
Purpose or Occasion: Merchandising
Number of Colors: 3

Design Firm: ZEDWEAR
All Design: John Klaja
Client: ZEDWEAR
Purpose or Occasion: Retail
Number of Colors: 2

The *Champion Breed* emblem was printed on
micro-stripe T-shirts and is part of the design
company's dalmatian-inspired sportswear.

WE'VE GOT ALL THE BRANDS YOU NEED.

1993 CESSNA PARTS MANAGERS MEETING
MILLER AVIATION

◀

Design Firm: Cerretani Design

All Design: Janet Cerretani

Client: Miller Aviation

Purpose or Occasion: Parts managers meeting

Number of Colors: 4

A promotional piece for an aircraft company's extensive parts department.

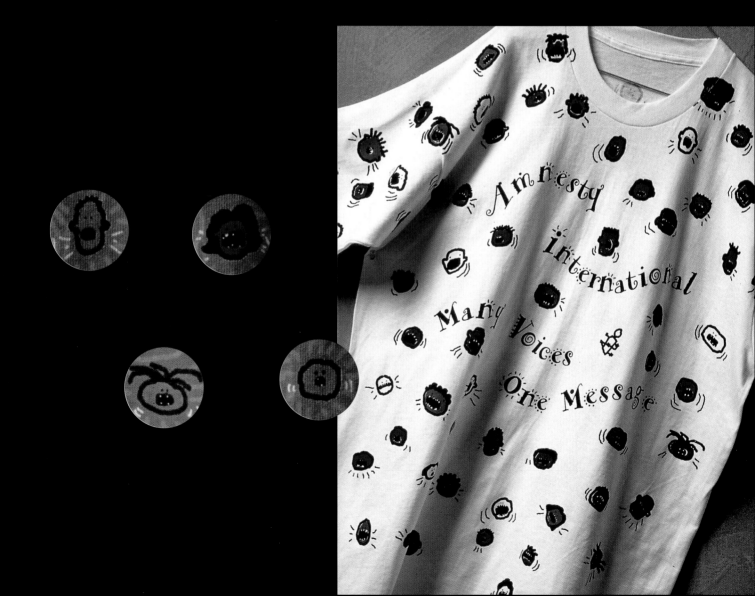

◄ ▲

Design Firm: Cliff Selbert Design/Mirror Image, Inc.

All Design: Lynn Riddle

Client: Amnesty International

Purpose or Occasion: International Council Meeting

Number of Colors: 4

Developed for Amnesty International's policy-making
conference, these T-shirts are also used as promotional items.

▶

Design Firm: Callahan & Co. Advertising
Art Director: Paula Sloane
Designers: Paula Sloane, Michael Crampton
Illustrator: Michael Crampton
Client: Callahan & Co. Advertising
Purpose or Occasion: Self promotion
Number of Colors: 3
Illustration spells out "C&C@9W.29th St."

▲

Design Firm: Sayles Graphic Design
All Design: John Sayles
Client: Beaverdale Neighborhood Association
Purpose or Occasion: Promotion
Number of Colors: 1
This friendly beaver character is the mascot
for the Beaverdale Neighborhood Association.
The T-shirt is sold in a box decorated with
the same logo.

▼

Design Firm: Sayles Graphic Design
All Design: John Sayles
Client: The Des Moines Art Center
Purpose or Occasion: Event staff identification
Number of Colors: 3

TENTH ANNUAL BAY2BAY INTERNATIONAL ROWING AND PADDLING REGATTA

▲

Design Firm: Mires Design, Inc.

Art Director: Jose Serrano

Designer: Jose Serrano

Illustrator: Gerald Bustamante

Client: Peninsula Family YMCA

Purpose or Occasion: Rowing regatta

Number of Colors: 4

◀ ▲

Design Firm: Richards and Swensen, Inc.
All Design: William Swensen
Client: Utah Symphony
Purpose or Occasion: Labor Day 5K run
Number of Colors: 5

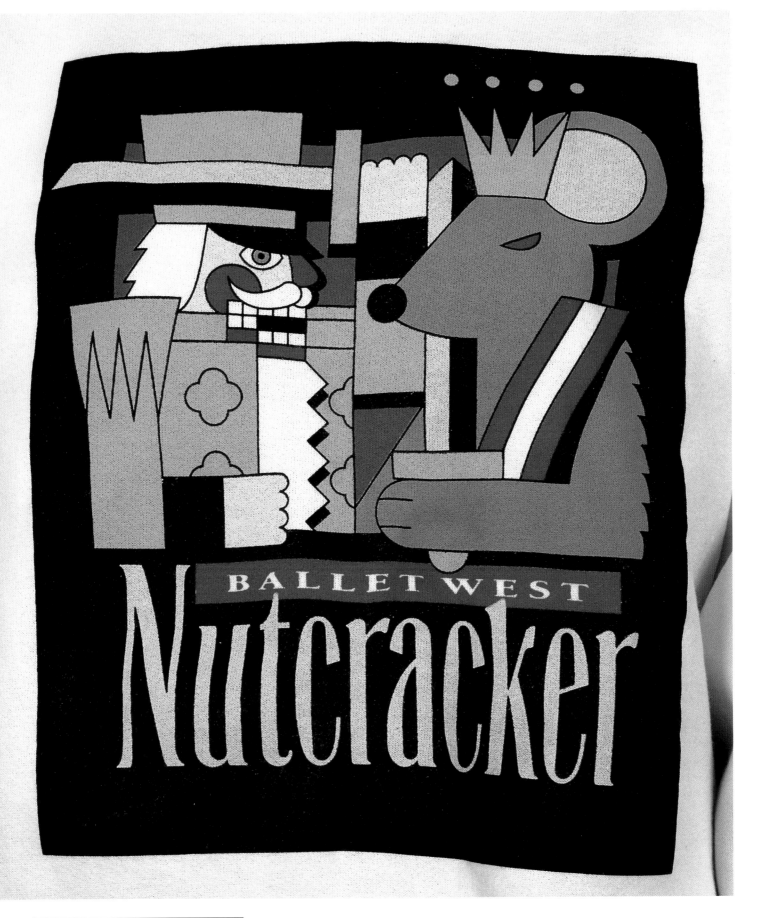

Design Firm: Richards and Swensen, Inc.

All Design: William Swensen

Client: Ballet West

Purpose or Occasion: Retail

Number of Colors: 6

Sweatshirt designed in conjunction with the
yearly performance of *The Nutcracker*.

BULL TERRIER CLUB OF DALLAS

1993 SPECIALTY

Design Firm: Sibley Peteet Design
Art Directors: John Evans, Don Sibley
Designer: John Evans
Illustrator: John Evans
Client: Bull Terrier Club of Dallas
Purpose or Occasion: Dog Show Award
Number of Colors: 4

◄

Design Firm: Supon Design Group, Inc.
Art Directors: Supon Phornirunlit, Jacque Coughlin
Designer: Steven Morris
Illustrator: Steven Morris
Client: Wolf Trap
Purpose or Occasion: Merchandising
Number of Colors: 4

►

Design Firm: Sayles Graphic Design
All Design: John Sayles
Client: The Des Moines Art Center
Purpose or Occasion: Fund-raiser
Number of Colors: 3

◄

Design Firm: Entheos Design
Designer: Debbie Dejno
Client: North Central Conference
Purpose or Occasion: Conference for youth
Number of Colors: 3

Designed for a conference theme, "Raising Up the Next Generation", this T-shirt design uses *halal*, the hebrew word for praise, boast, or celebrate. The shirt appeals to both young and old and has been reprinted.

Design Firm: Sportdecals
All Design: Sportdecals
Client: Assorted schools
Purpose or Occasion: Promotion
Number of Colors: 2

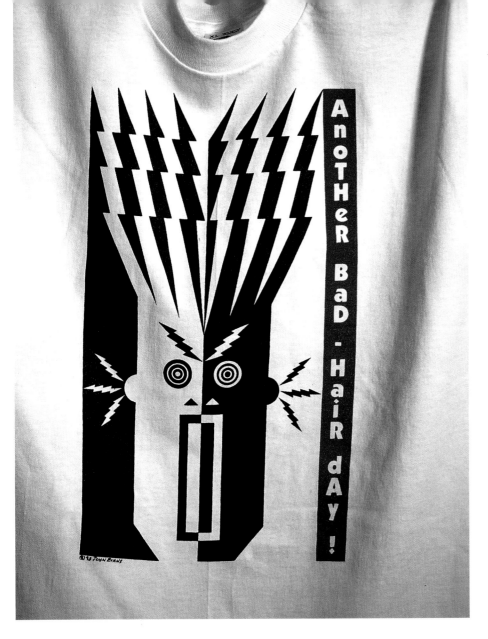

◀

Design Firm: John Evans Design
All Design: John Evans
Purpose or Occasion: Retail
Number of Colors: 2

▼

Design Firm: Art Guy Studios
Art Director: James F. Kraus
Designer: James F. Kraus
Illustrator: James F. Kraus
Client: WZBC 90.3 FM
Purpose or Occasion: Begathon premium
Number of Colors: 1

▲

Design Firm: Art Guy Studios
Art Directors: James F. Kraus, Boomer Kenedy
Designer: James F. Kraus
Illustrator: James F. Kraus
Client: Chicago Auto
Purpose or Occasion: Retail
Number of Colors: 1

▶
Design Firm: Segura Inc.
All Design: Carlos Segura
Client: [T-26]
Purpose or Occasion: Promotion
Number of Colors: 2

◀ ▼
Design Firm: SullivanPerkins
Art Directors: Ron Sullivan, Kelly Allen
Designer: Kelly Allen
Illustrator: Kelly Allen
Client: Meltzer & Martin Public Realtors
Purpose or Occasion: Third Anniversary of Meltzer & Martin
Number of Colors: 4

◀

Design Firm: Sackett Design
Art Director: Mark Sackett
Designers: Mark Sackett, Wayne Sakamoto
Client: Levi Strauss & Co.—*Little Levi's*
Purpose or Occasion: Promotion
Number of Colors: 2 and 3
These T-shirts promote *Little Levi's*, a new line of clothing for children aged 4-6.

▶

Design Firm: Sackett Design
All Design: Mark Sackett
Client: Mervyn's IMI Apparel
Purpose or Occasion: Promotion
Number of Colors: 3 and 4
These T-shirts promote a new line of apparel for young girls.

Design Firm: The Riordon Design Group, Inc.

Art Director: Ric Riordon

Illustrator: Dan Wheaton

Client: Toronto Sick Kids Hospital

Purpose or Occasion: CFTO-TV telethon

Number of Colors: 7

Produced to give-away to telethon contributors, this T-shirt helped raise funds for Sick Kids Hospital.

Design Firm: Reliv, Inc.
All Design: Jay Smith
Client: Reliv, Inc.
Purpose or Occasion: Contest winner give-away
Number of Colors: 5
The Maui T-shirt was given to 50 contest winners internationally.

Design Firm: Elton Ward Design
All Design: Jason Dominiak
Client: Ray Ban
Purpose or Occasion: Promotional give-away
Number of Colors: 4

T-shirt graphic for *Predator* series of sunglasses.

Design Firm: Speak, Inc.
All Design: Amy Cahill, Chele Isaac
Client: Speak, Inc.
Purpose or Occasion: Retail

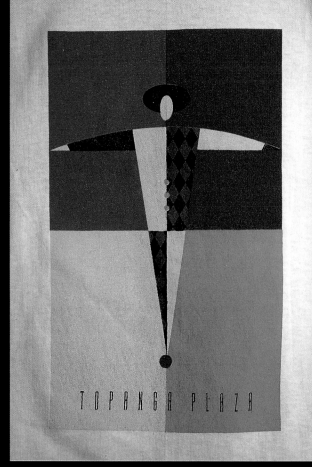

Design Firm: Jon Flaming Design
All Design: Jon Flaming
Client: Ken Knight
Purpose or Occasion: Retail
Number of Colors: 3

▲

Design Firm: SullivanPerkins
Art Directors: Jon Flaming, Ron Sullivan
Designer: Jon Flaming
Illustrator: Jon Flaming
Client: Topanga Plaza
Purpose or Occasion: Promotion
Number of Colors: 6

YEEHAAAA!, Y'ALL!

DALLAS

▲

Design Firm: The Riordon Design Group, Inc.

Art Director: Ric Riordon

Designer: Dan Wheaton

Illustrator: Dan Wheaton

Client: Service Master Canada

Purpose or Occasion: Corporate performance premium

Number of Colors: 7

▶

Design Firm: Joan C. Hollingsworth

All Design: Joan C. Hollingsworth

Client: Joan C. Hollingsworth

Purpose or Occasion: Gift for artist's
grandchildren

Number of Colors: 4

Design Firm: Ken Brown Designs
Designer: Ken Brown
Purpose or Occasion: Retail
Number of Colors: 6

Design Firm: Dean Johnson Design

All Design: Bruce Dean

Client: Some Guys Pizza

Purpose or Occasion: Retail

Number of Colors: 4

A series of shirts using images of famous paintings
altered with the client's logo or a picture of a pizza
added to the scene.

▲

Design Firm: Mires Design, Inc.
All Design: John Ball
Production: Miguel Perez
Client: California Center for the Arts, Escondido
Purpose or Occasion: Promotion
Number of Colors: 2

▶

Design Firm: John Fleming Design
All Design: Jon Fleming
Client: Baker & McKenzie
Purpose or Occasion: 10K run
Number of Colors: 4

1

Humane Society of Ramsey County

K9-5k

Eighth Annual

2

THE **COPPER GRID**

BAR & GRILL

MADISON

4

COUNTRY

J A M

QUEEN CREEK, ARIZONA

5

POLKA LIVES

OKTOBERFEST•USA

L A C R O S S E

7

OKTOBERFEST USA

ROLL OUT THE BARREL!

L A C R O S S E

8

F L E T C H E R ' S

WHARF

LAKE MINNETONKA

Design Firm: Creative Pig Minds
All Design: Brian D. Endl

I
Client: Ramsey County Humane Society, St. Paul, MN
Purpose or Occasion: 5K run/walk to benefit Humane Society
Number of Colors: 4

2
Client: Copper Grid Bar & Grill
Purpose or Occasion: Retail
Number of Colors: 3

3
Client: Vegetarians in Motion
Purpose or Occasion: For sale to members
Number of Colors: 5

4
Client: Country Jam USA
Purpose or Occasion: Retail
Number of Colors: 6

5
Client: Oktoberfest USA LaCrosse, WI
Purpose or Occasion: Retail
Number of Colors: 5

6
Client: Oktoberfest USA LaCrosse, WI
Purpose or Occasion: Retail
Number of Colors: 5

7
Client: Oktoberfest USA LaCrosse, WI
Purpose or Occasion: Retail
Number of Colors: 5

8
Client: Fletcher's Wharf Bar
Purpose or Occasion: Promotion & retail
Number of Colors: 4

9
Client: Brothers In Law Bar
Purpose or Occasion: Promotion & retail
Number of Colors: 4

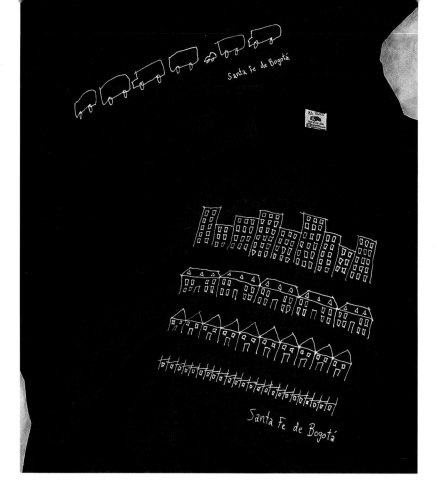

Design Firm: Ricardo Beron Castro
All Design: Ricardo Beron Castro
Purpose or Occasion: Retail
Number of Colors: 1

Design Firm: The Design Company
Art Director: Marcia Romanuck
Designers: Marcia Romanuck, Denise Pickering
Client: The Design Company
Purpose or Occasion: Christmas gift
Number of Colors: 1

FRANK LLOYD WRIGHT

FALLINGWATER
THE EDGAR J. KAUFMANN HOUSE
MILL RUN, PENNSYLVANIA, 1935
©1993 THE FRANK LLOYD WRIGHT FOUNDATION

FRANK LLOYD WRIGHT ®

Design Firm: Fotofolio/Mirror Image, Inc.
Art Director: Ron Schick
Designer: Frank Lloyd Wright
Client: Fotofolio
Purpose or Occasion: Retail
Number of Colors: 7
Separations/Printing: Mirror Image, Inc./
Judy Winters

Design Firm: Lehner & Whyte

Art Directors: Donna Lehner, Hugh Whyte

Designers: Hugh Whyte, Donna Lehner

Illustrator: Hugh Whyte

Client: FX4U Zoo

Purpose or Occasion: Retail

Number of Colors: 4

FX4U™

ZOO

Design Firm: Lehner & Whyte

Art Directors: Donna Lehner, Hugh Whyte

Designers: Hugh Whyte, Donna Lehner

Illustrator: Hugh Whyte

Client: FX4U Zoo

Purpose or Occasion: Retail

Number of Colors: 5

©MCMXCIV HEARTLAND APPAREL

Design Firm: Heartland Apparel

Art Director: Kathy Berwald

Designer: Johnny Wilson

Illustrator: Johnny Wilson

Client: Custom

Purpose or Occasion: Souvenir retail

Number of Colors: 6

SAN DIEGO ZOO

SAN DIEGO WILD ANIMAL PARK

◄

Design Firm: Barbara Ferguson Designs
All Design: Barbara Ferguson
Client: Zoological Society of San Diego
Purpose or Occasion: Merchandising
Number of Colors: 5

▼

Design Firm: High Cotton, Inc.
All Design: Kathryn Glick
Client: High Cotton, Inc.
Purpose or Occasion: Retail
Number of Colors: 5

"GOODNIGHT"

Design Firm: PandaMonium Design
Art Director: Raymond Yu
Designer: Raymond Yu
Illustrators: Cathy Greve, Terry Stangel
Client: Restaurant Concepts, Inc.
Purpose or Occasion: Promotion
Number of Colors: 4

Design Firm: Bi Bi Dee
Client: Basic Publications
Purpose or Occasion: Custom orders
Number of Colors: 4

Design Firm: Sibley Peteet Design
All Design: John Evans
Client: Spirit Cruises
Purpose or Occasion: Retail
Number of Colors: 4

Design Firm: 90° Angle
All Design: Kim Sager
Client: Four Seasons Hotel & Resort
Purpose or Occasion: Retail
Number of Colors: 9

ISLAND PACKET YACHTS®

RENDEZVOUS 1994

ROCK HALL MARYLAND

WILLIAM WEGMAN

LOLITA, 1990 © 1994 WILLIAM WEGMAN, FOTOFOLIO

Design Firm: Fotofolio/Mirror Image
Art Director: Ron Schick
Color Separator: Colin Cheer
Designer: William Wegman
Photographer: William Wegman
Client: Fotofolio
Purpose or Occasion: Retail
Number of Colors: 5

©1994 ZEDWEAR

◀

Design Firm: ZEDWEAR
Art Director: John Klaja
Designer: John Klaja
Illustrator: John Klaja
Client: ZEDWEAR
Purpose or Occasion: Retail
Number of Colors: 2
Printer: Tasty Shirt Company

This *Good Dog* design expands the ZEDWEAR line with a series of T-shirts featuring images inspired by "Zed", the owner's dalmatian.

Team Bone Tail Chasing

Redbone ALLEY

Tail Chasing Team

▲

Design Firm: Gil Shuler Graphic Design, Inc.
Art Director: Gil Shuler
Designers: Gil Shuler, Steve Lepre
Illustrator: Gil Shuler
Client: Redbone Alley Restaurant
Purpose or Occasion: Merchandising
Number of Colors: 2

▲

Design Firm: Hon Blue Inc.

All Design: Keith Sasaki

Client: Jalapeno Henry's

Purpose or Occasion: Chili cook-off

Number of Colors: 4

Organizers chose a Native American theme for
their chili cook-off contest, which is reflected in
this shirt design. Although many people wanted
to buy this T-shirt, only enough had been made for
the cook-off team.

CHILI PEPPER

Herbal Tees © By Kim for 90° Angle

(Capsicum)
Ruling Planet: MARS
ELEMENT: FIRE
POWERS: LUST, MONEY, WEALTH

MAGICAL USES:
RED PEPPER WILL
ENSURE that the love
YOU FIND WILL be spicy.

Design Firm: 90° Angle
All Design: Kim Sager
Client: 90° Angle
Purpose or Occasion: Retail
Number of Colors: 5
This shirt, created for the *Herbal Tee* series, appeals
to both men and women.

▲

Design Firm: Scoville Creative
All Design: Laura Scoville
Client: Spectrum Center for Integrated Care
Purpose or Occasion: Aids Walk Chicago
Number of Colors: 3
Printer: Propaganda

This T-shirt won the "impact" prize out of more than 30 entries from all the corporate sponsors and teams. Its indigo color made the team stand out, while its printed message inspired dialogue.

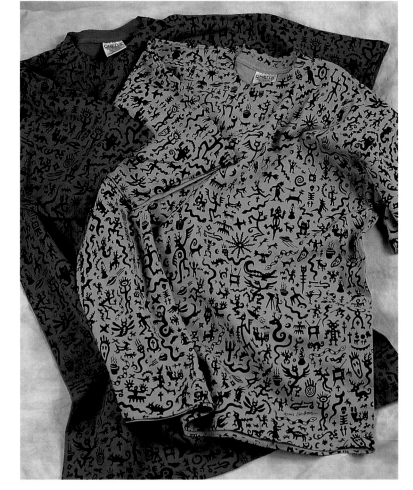

▶

Design Firm: Ken Brown
Designer: Ken Brown
Purpose or Occasion: Retail
Number of Colors: 1

◄

Design Firm: K.E. Roehr Design/Illustration
All Design: K.E. Roehr
Client: Pan Mass Challenge/Jimmy Fund
Purpose or Occasion: Honor participants
Number of Colors: 5

This T-shirt was given to cyclists who raised over $1,500 for the Jimmy Fund and earned the title "Heavy Hitter." The *Miracles Can Happen* theme was used because although rain had been predicted for the annual 2-day 192-mile ride, the weather was perfect!

▼

Art Director: Dave Parmley
Designer: Sandy Gin
Client: O'Neill, Inc.
Purpose or Occasion: Retail
Number of Colors: 6

Design Firm: Mires Design, Inc.
Art Director: Jose Serrano
Designers: Jose Serrano, Mike Brower
Client: Baldwin
Purpose or Occasion: Baseball team uniform
Number of Colors: 1

1993 DCCCD COMMERCIAL

To bee or not to bee.

BUZZ

Design Firm: Gibbs Baronet
Art Directors: Willie Baronet, Steve Gibbs
Designers: Tammy Yarlagadda, Willie Baronet
Client: Dallas County Community College District
Purpose or Occasion: Give-away for actors used in a television commercial for Dallas County Community College District
Number of Colors: 2

Design Firm: Ken Brown Designs
Designer: Ken Brown
Purpose or Occasion: Retail
Number of Colors: 3

Design Firm: Charney Design
All Design: Carol Inez Charney
Client: Borland
Purpose or Occasion: Give-away
Number of Colors: 4

This give-away T-shirt was designed as a cross between *The Nature Company* and the periodic table of the elements. Targeted at Beta testers, people who look for bugs in software, the shirt design uses real bugs and lots of artistic license.

Design Firm: PandaMonium Designs
Art Director: Raymond Yu
Designers: Raymond Yu, Steven Yee
Illustrator: Steven Lee
Client: Technique
Purpose or Occasion: Promotion
Number of Colors: 7

◀

Design Firm: Cerretani Design
All Design: Janet Cerretani
Client: Miller Aviation
Purpose or Occasion: Give-away
Number of Colors: 3

Promotional T-shirt for an air transportation trade show.

▶

Design Firm: Pictogram Studio
Art Director: Stephanie Hooton
Designers: Hien Nguyen, Stephanie Hooton
Illustrator: Hien Nguyen
Client: Capital Tees
Purpose or Occasion: Summer promotion
Number of Colors: 2

◀

Design Firm: Sayles Graphic Design
All Design: John Sayles
Client: American Institute of Architects
Purpose or Occasion: Promotion & commemoration
Number of Colors: 3

A promotion for an annual sandcastle-building contest.

Design Firm: Barbara Ferguson, Lee Merrill
Art Directors: Barbara Ferguson,
Lee Merrill
Designers: Barbara Ferguson, Lee Merrill
Illustrator: Barbara Ferguson
Client: Zoological Society of San Diego
Purpose or Occasion: Celebration of
the dinosaur exhibit
Number of Colors: 5

Design Firm: Lehner & Whyte
Art Directors: Donna Lehner, Hugh Whyte
Designers: Hugh Whyte, Donna Lehner
Illustrator: Hugh Whyte
Client: Lehner & Whyte
Purpose or Occasion: Holiday self-promotion
Number of Colors: 5

Design Firm: PandaMonium Designs
Art Director: Raymond Yu
Designers: Raymond Yu, Daniel Yee
Client: KA-BOOM! Sportswear
Purpose or Occasion: Retail
Number of Colors: 3
Shirts were designed to celebrate the August
Moon Festival, an annual cultural event in
Boston's Chinatown.

AUGUST
MOON
festival

Boston Chinatown

AUGUST
MOON
FESTIVAL

BOSTON
chinatown

Design Firm: Mike Salisbury Communications
All Design: Mike Salisbury
Client: GOTCHA
Purpose or Occasion: Retail
Number of Colors: 5

Design Firm: Mike Salisbury Communications
Art Director: Mike Salisbury
Designer: Terry Lamb
Illustrator: Terry Lamb
Client: GOTCHA
Purpose or Occasion: Retail
Number of Colors: 4

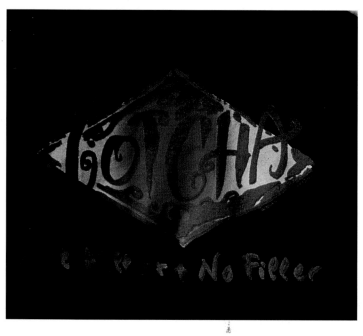

Design Firm: Mike Salisbury Communications
Art Director: Mike Salisbury
Designer: Damion Gallay
Illustrator: Damion Gallay
Client: GOTCHA
Purpose or Occasion: Retail
Number of Colors: 4

Design Firm: Mike Salisbury Communications
Art Director: Mike Salisbury
Designers: Terry Lamb, Mike Salisbury
Illustrators: Terry Lamb, Mike Salisbury
Client: GOTCHA
Purpose or Occasion: Retail
Number of Colors: 7

Design Firm: Mike Salisbury
Communications
Art Director: Mike Salisbury
Designer: Terry Lamb
Illustrator: Terry Lamb
Client: GOTCHA
Purpose or Occasion: Retail
Number of Colors: 6

▼ ▶

Design Firm: Russell Leong Design
Art Director: Russell K. Leong
Designer: Russell K. Leong
Illustrator: Michael Schawb
Client: Sun Microsystems
Purpose or Occasion: World
Cup Soccer
Number of Colors: 5

▶

Design Firm: Russell Leong Design
Art Director: Russell K. Leong
Designer: Russell K. Leong
Illustrator: Michael Schawb
Client: Sun Microsystems
Purpose or Occasion: World
Cup Soccer
Number of Colors: 4

Design Firm: Sportdecals
All Design: Sportdecals
Client: Assorted schools
Purpose or Occasion: Promotion
Number of Colors: 3

▲

Design Firm: Rickabaugh Graphics

All Design: Eric Rickabaugh

Client: Ohio State University Athletics Dept.

Purpose or Occasion: Twenty-fifth anniversary of Ohio State University football National Championship

Number of Colors: 4

▲

Design Firm: Sayles Graphic Design

All Design: John Sayles

Client: Vermeet Manufacturing

Purpose or Occasion: Employee incentive

Number of Colors: 4

Presented in a custom-designed can, this shirt was given to Vermeet Manufacturing employees at an annual event.

Design Firm: X-Design Co.
Art Director: Alex Valderama
Designer: Alex Valderama
Illustrator: Doug Applegate
Client: Farrell's U.S. Martial Arts
Purpose or Occasion: Annual Tae Kwon Do tournament
Number of Colors: 3

▼

Design Firm: Pentagram Design
Art Director: Peter Hamson
Designers: Kevin Lauterbach, Steve Purtill
Client: American Institute of Graphic Arts, New York
Purpose or Occasion: Tenth anniversary gift for members
Number of Colors: 2

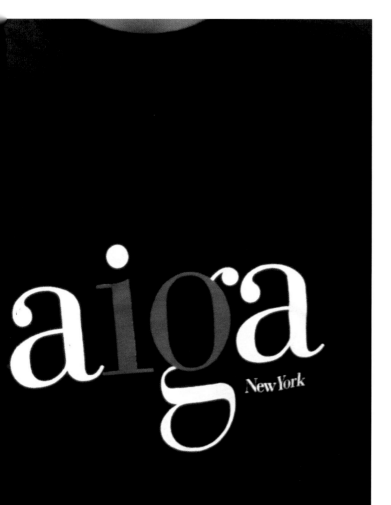

▲

Design Firm: High Cotton, Inc.
Art Director: Tim Doughtie
Designer: Michael Meissner
Client: High Cotton, Inc.
Purpose or Occasion: Retail
Number of Colors: 2

▼

Design Firm: Sommese Design
All Design: Lanny Sommese
Client: Joel Confer Softball Team
Purpose or Occasion: Team jersey
Number of Colors: 2

Design Firm: Lania Ink, Inc.
All Design: John R. Patton
Client: Lania Ink, Inc.
Purpose or Occasion: Cultural theme awareness
Number of Colors: 6

The petroglyphs and pictographs that decorate this T-shirt are a permanent record of the traditions and the roots of image-making in the Marianas Islands.

Design Firm: Sommese Design
All Design: Lanny Sommese
Client: Joel Confer Softball Team
Purpose or Occasion: Team jersey
Number of Colors: 2

Design Firm: Mike Salisbury
Communications
All Design: Mike Salisbury
Client: Birdwell
Purpose or Occasion: Promotion
Number of Colors: 4

Design Firm: Applegate Art & Design
All Design: Doug Applegate
Client: Applegate Art and Design
Purpose or Occasion: Self-promotion
Number of Colors: 2

Tongue Twisters For Braces!

Thister thuzy thells thea thells by the thea thore!

Who needs Cable...

when you have Braces!

I'm not Smiling...

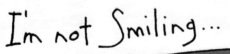

My lips are just hung-up on my Braces!

When you wear braces...

Curling your hair can be electrifying!

▲

Design Firm: Barb-Wire Designs
All Design: Barbara Ferguson
Client: Barb-Wire Designs
Purpose or Occasion: Retail
Number of Colors: 6

A series of T-shirt designs depicting the hazards of wearing braces.

◄

Design Firm: The Bon Marché
Art Director: Jean DeLatyree
Designer: Jean DeLatyree
Illustrator: Ken Shafer
Client: The Bon Marche
Purpose or Occasion: "Mom and me at the zoo"
Number of Colors: 2

Design Firm: Marlene Montgomery Design
All Design: Marlene Montgomery
Client: Marlene Montgomery Design
Purpose or Occasion: Retail
Number of Colors: 2

Part computer generated, part hand cut, this T-shirt design is reminiscent of the many letters that are exchanged between lovers.

Design Firm: Gibbs Baronet
Art Directors: Steve Gibbs, Willie Baronet
Designers: Steve Gibbs, Tammy Yarlagadda
Client: AIDS Arms
Purpose or Occasion: Promotion of "AIDS Arms" and display of new logo.
Number of Colors: 2

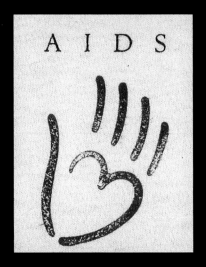

▲

Design Firm: Marlene Montgomery Design
All Design: Marlene Montgomery
Client: Marlene Montgomery Design
Purpose or Occasion: Retail
Number of Colors: 2

◀

Design Firm: Pictogram Studio
Art Director: Stephanie Hooton
Designers: Hien Nguyen, Stephanie Hooton
Illustrator: Hien Nguyen
Client: Pictogram Studio
Purpose or Occasion: Valentine's Day
Number of Colors: 1

"Tried By His Pears-II"

"... red sky at night, watermelon de-light!"

"Seeds and Stripes Forever"

I Wedge Allegiance!

▲

Design Firm: Ogre's Alley
All Design: David J. Ogorzaly
Client: Friends, relatives, and business associates
Purpose or Occasion: Retail
The original artwork for this T-shirt was designed using colored pencils. The designer prints his watermelon art on *Fruit of the Loom* products, using laser color copier heat transfer.

▲

Design Firm: Ogre's Alley
All Design: David J. Ogorzaly
Client: Friends, relatives, and business associates
Purpose or Occasion: Retail
"I Wedge Allegiance/Seeds & Stripes Forever" fulfills the demand for having a two-sided T-shirt design. The "wedge" on the breast pocket makes viewers giggle a little—but the total concept comes to life when the watermelon flag is viewed on the back side of the T-shirt.

True Colors
THE ALL-AMERICAN ART SHOW
LANGUAGE HOUSE GALLERY, CHICAGO • OCTOBER 14th 1994

◄

Design Firm: Propaganda
Art Director: Jason Meadows
Designer: Lowell Thompson
Client: Partnership Against Racism
Purpose or Occasion: Promotion of an art show
Number of Colors: 6

►

Design Firm: Alphawave Design
All Design: Douglas Dunebin
Client: Alphawave/Buck the System Foundation
Purpose or Occasion: Retail
Number of Colors: 4

◄

Design Firm: The Design Company
All Design: Marcia Romanuck
Client: The Design Company
Purpose or Occasion: Gift
Number of Colors: 2

▶

Design Firm: Aardvark Graphics
Art Director: Bobby Griffiths
Designer: Johnny Wilson
Illustrator: Johnny Wilson
Client: Minnesota Zoo
Purpose or Occasion: Minnesota Zoo
"Bugs" exhibit
Number of Colors: 5

ZOOKEEPERS

◄

Design Firm: Jon Flaming Design
All Design: Jon Flaming
Client: The Dallas Zoo
Purpose or Occasion: Fund-raiser
Number of Colors: 4

▶

Design Firm: Joss Design Group
All Design: Timothy Stebbing
Client: Joss Design Group
Purpose or Occasion: Self-promotion
Number of Colors: 3
A calligraphic play with the letter "J" of *Joss Design Group*, the image of the Hancock Building that dominates the Chicago skyline, and the colors of the *Joss* logo were used in this design.

Design Firm: Crabtree & Strussion Design
Art Director: Richard Crabtree
Designer: Lauraine Strussion
Illustrator: Lauraine Strussion
Client: Squire Limited for Men
Purpose or Occasion: Thank-you gift for clients
Number of Colors: 2

DREAM YOUR DREAMS

find a way

Imagine the possibilities

© 1993 JOED DESIGN INC.

Design Firm: JOED Design Inc.
Art Director: Edward Rebek
Designers: Edward Rebek, Joanne Rebek
Client: JOED Design Inc.
Purpose or Occasion: Self-promotion
Number of Colors: 2

The natural cotton "Dream Your Dreams" T-shirt features green/black duotone images.

Design Firm: Mires Design, Inc.
Art Director: Jose Serrano
Designer: Jose Serrano
Illustrator: Dan Thoner

▲

Design Firm: Jon Flaming Design
All Design: Jon Flaming
Client: Michael O. & Associates, Inc.
Purpose or Occasion: Promotion
Number of Colors: 2

▼

Art Director: Dave Parmley
Designer: Sandy Gin
Client: O'Neill, Inc.
Purpose or Occasion: Retail
Number of Colors: 2

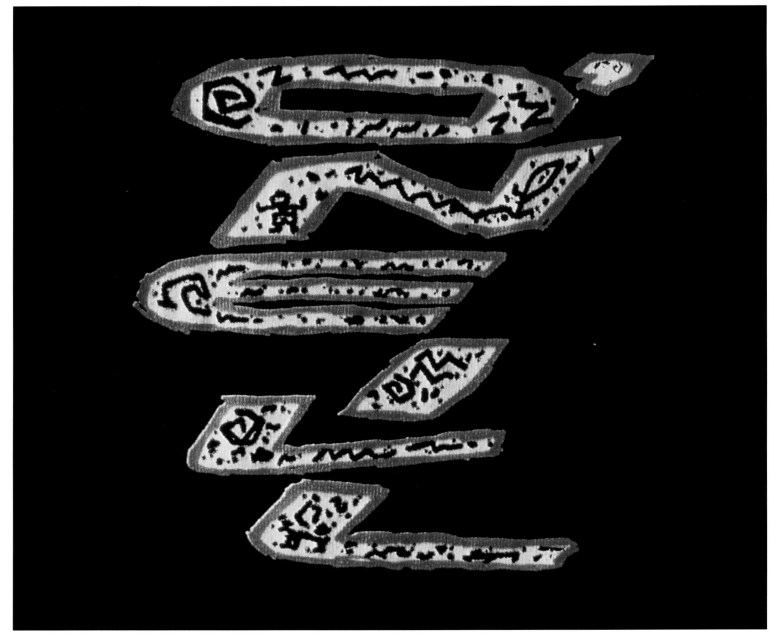

Design Firm: Blue Chicago

Art Director: Gino Battagia

Designer: Gino Battagia

Illustrator: John C. Doyle

Client: Blue Chicago

Purpose or Occasion: Retail

Number of Colors: 10

Design Firm: Sackett Design
Art Director: Mark Sackett
Designers: Mark Sackett, Wayne Sakamoto
Illustrators: Mark Sackett,
Wayne Sakamoto
Client: DFS Group - Texas project
Purpose or Occasion: Retail
Number of Colors: 4 and 3
This series of "destination" T-shirts were designed
for Texas- and Houston-based gift stores.

Design Firm: A. Kaligos & Co.
All Design: Nick Kaligos
Purpose or Occasion: Retail
Number of Colors: 4

◄

Design Firm: Supon Design Group, Inc.
Art Directors: Supon Phornirunlit,
Jacque Coughlin
Designer: Mimi Eanes
Illustrator: Mimi Eanes
Client: George Meany Center for Labor Studies
Purpose or Occasion: Premium give-away
Number of Colors: 4

T-shirt was designed to commemorate the twenty-fifth anniversary of the George Meany Center.

▶

Design Firm: RIP Ink.
All Design: Tabatha Cottrell
Client: The Public in Need
Purpose or Occasion: Retail
Number of Colors: 2

Another version of the *Yes! Lenny!* design, with colors manipulated by the artist.

Design Firm: Lehner & Whyte
Art Directors: Donna Lehner, Hugh Whyte
Designers: Hugh Whyte, Donna Lehner
Illustrator: Hugh Whyte
Client: FX4U
Purpose or Occasion: Retail
Number of Colors: 1

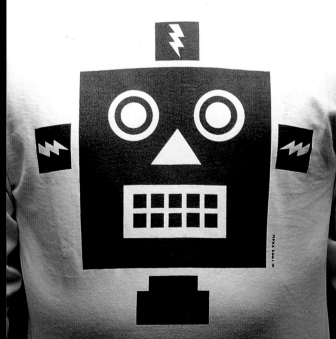

▲

Design Firm: Mires Design, Inc.

Art Director: John Ball

Designer: John Ball

Production: Miguel Perez

Client: California Center for the Arts, Escondido

Purpose or Occasion: Promotion

Number of Colors: 1

The T-shirt's *Art & Soul* logo promotes the grand opening of the Center for Visual and Performing Arts.

▶

Design Firm: Lee Reedy Design Associates

All Design: Lee Reedy

Client: MCI

Purpose or Occasion: Employee incentive program

Number of Colors: 1

This oversized, knee-length shirt was used as a promotional incentive to MCI's telemarketers. The campaign theme was "Big" and all of the pieces were oversized.

◀

Design Firm: Dyer/Mutchnick Group, Inc.

Art Director: Rod Dyer

Designer: Clive Piercy

Client: Spuntino Restaurant

Purpose or Occasion: Promotion

Number of Colors: 10

▶

Design Firm: Russell Leong Design

All Design: Russell K. Leong

Client: E-MU Systems

Purpose or Occasion: Promotion

Number of Colors: 4

Design Firm:	Mirror Image, Inc.
Art Director:	Erica Reitmayer
Designer:	Derek Yesman
Client:	Great Woods
Purpose or Occasion:	Promotion & retail
Number of Colors:	5

◀

Design Firm: Sibley Peteet Design
All Design: John Evans
Client: National Kidney Foundation
Purpose or Occasion: 10K run
Number of Colors: 4

▶

Design Firm: Lee Reedy Design Associates
All Design: Lee Reedy
Client: American Water Works Association
Purpose or Occasion: Promotion
Number of Colors: 2
This design promotes National Drinking Water Week
and the protection of clean drinking water.

Give drinking water a hand.

9TH ANNUAL PLANO

BALLOON FESTIVAL

Design Firm: SullivanPerkins
Art Directors: Ron Sullivan, Art Garcia
Designer: Art Garcia
Client: Plano Balloon Festival Committee
Purpose or Occasion: Ninth annual
Plano Balloon Festival
Number of Colors: 5

Design Firm: John Evans Design
All Design: John Evans
Client: Deep Ellum Association
Purpose or Occasion: Fund-raiser
Number of Colors: 6

1994

DEEP ELLUM

Design Firm: Karyl Klopp Design
All Design: Karyl Klopp
Client: Martha Eliot Health Center
Purpose or Occasion: Promotion
Number of Colors: 5

Designed to express multiculturalism and a positive sense of life, this T-shirt was created for a men's group on sensitivity awareness.

Design Firm: Bullet Communications, Inc.

All Design: Tim Scott

Client: Information Resources, Inc.

Purpose or Occasion: Corporate challenge run

Number of Colors: 2

Design Firm: Lehner & Whyte

Art Directors: Donna Lehner, Hugh Whyte

Designers: Hugh Whyte, Donna Lehner

Illustrator: Hugh Whyte

Client: FX4U

Purpose or Occasion: Retail

Number of Colors: 4

▲

Design Firm: Fountainhead Advertising
All Design: Dory Colbert
Copywriter: Dory Colbert
Client: Grant Elementary School
Purpose or Occasion: Word of the Year
Number of Colors: 3

This shirt was a pro bono project to raise funds for Grant Elementary School. "Respect" was the school's "word of the year," and the design features multicultural design icons reflecting the diverse cultural base of the school.

▼

Design Firm: Walcott-Ayers Group
All Design: Jim Walcott-Ayers
Client: The Gathering at Big Fork
Purpose or Occasion: Fund-raiser
Number of Colors: 4

This sweatshirt was sold for a week-long workshop for playwrights and actors at Big Fork, Montana.

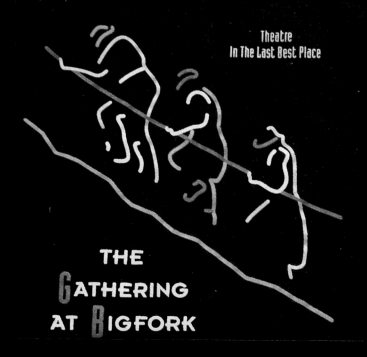

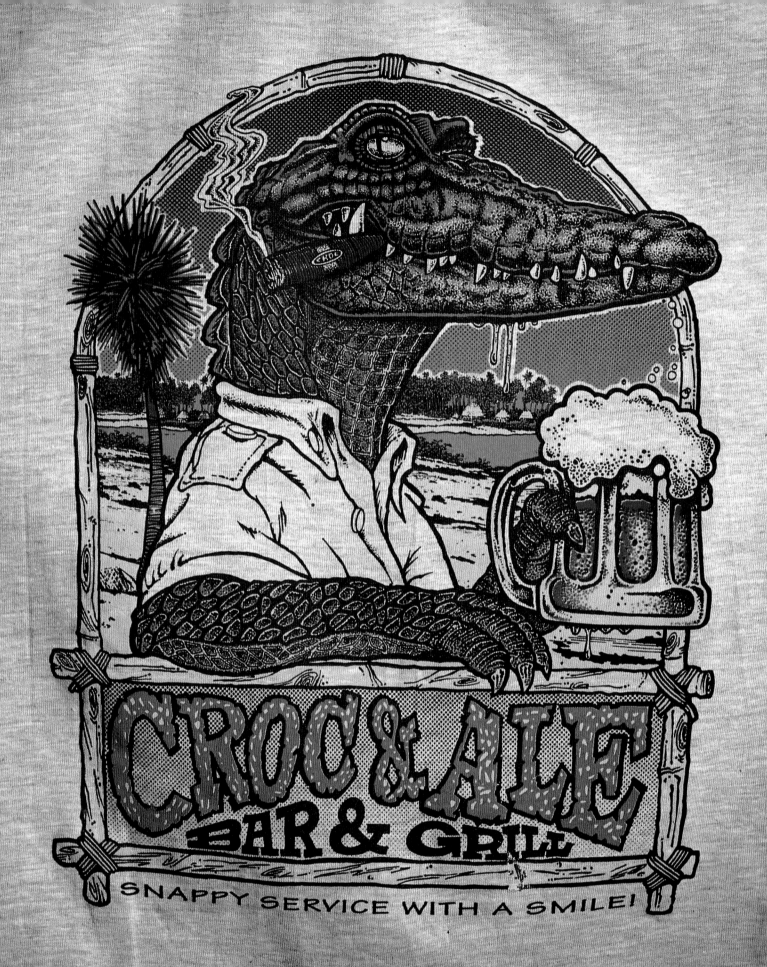

CROC & ALE
BAR & GRILL
SNAPPY SERVICE WITH A SMILE!

◀

Design Firm: Lee Tyin

Art Director: Maria Lee

Designer: Chris Yin

Illustrator: Chris Yin

Client: Semay, Inc.

Purpose or Occasion: Promotion

Number of Colors: 2

▶

Design Firm: Russell Leong Design

All Design: Russell K. Leong

Client: Intempo Toys

Purpose or Occasion: Celebrate the Arts

Number of Colors: 4

◀

Design Firm: Textile Printers Pty. Ltd.

Art Director: George Raimondo

Designer: George Raimondo

Illustrator: Richard Emery

Client: K-Mart

Purpose or Occasion: Retail

Number of Colors: 5

Design Firm: C. Benjamin Dacus
All Design: C. Benjamin Dacus
Client: Virginia Commonwealth University
Richmond, VA
Purpose or Occasion: Promotional souvenir
Number of Colors: 2

Design Firm: Lehner & Whyte
Art Directors: Donna Lehner, Hugh Whyte
Designers: Donna Lehner, Hugh Whyte
Illustrator: Hugh Whyte
Client: FX4U
Purpose or Occasion: Retail
Number of Colors: 2

Design Firm: Michael Kern Design

All Design: Michael Kern

Client: In-Motion, Inc.

Purpose or Occasion: Give-away

Number of Colors: 4

This T-shirt, designed to reflect the coastal course for the marathon, was given to runners who finished the race.

Design Firm: John Evans Design

All Design: John Evans

Purpose or Occasion: Retail

Number of Colors: 4

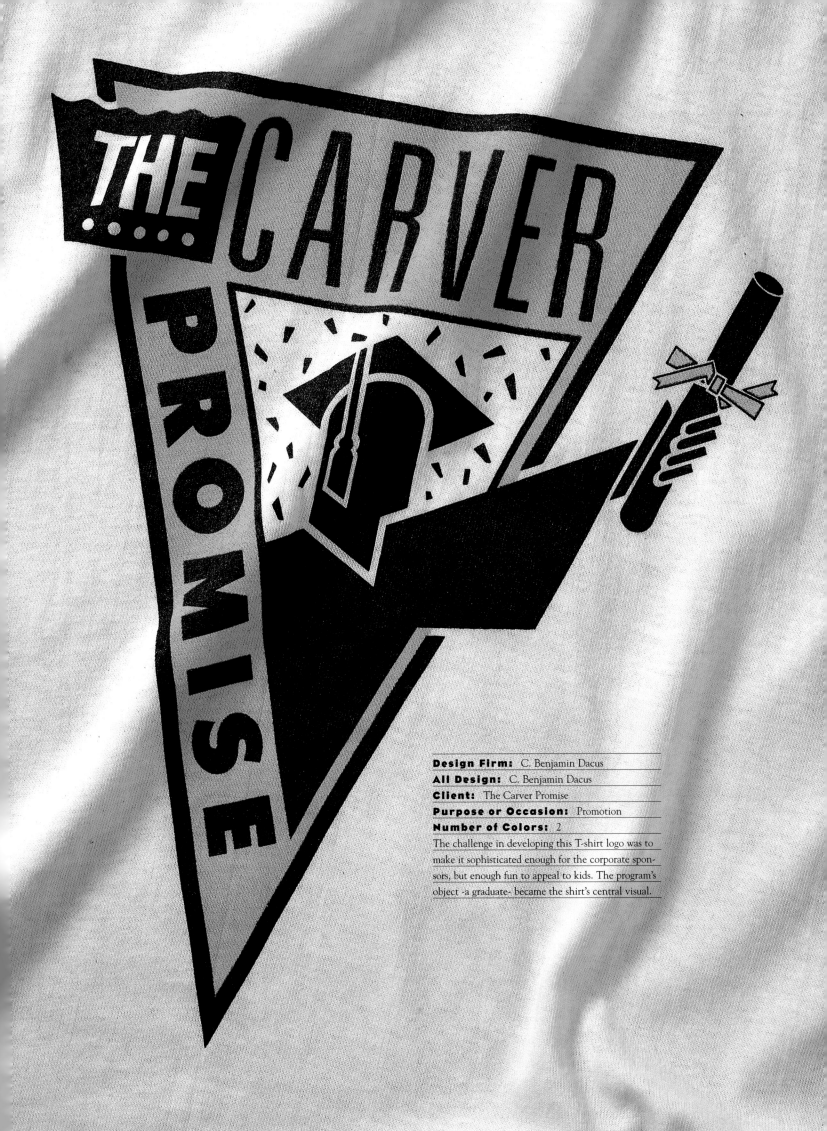

Design Firm: C. Benjamin Dacus

All Design: C. Benjamin Dacus

Client: The Carver Promise

Purpose or Occasion: Promotion

Number of Colors: 2

The challenge in developing this T-shirt logo was to make it sophisticated enough for the corporate sponsors, but enough fun to appeal to kids. The program's object -a graduate- became the shirt's central visual.

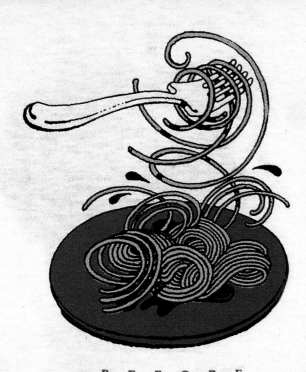

B E F O R E

50 MILE RACE SERIES
INDUSTRIAL SUPPY COMPANY
1 9 9 2

Design Firm: The Weller Institute For The Cure of Design

All Design: Don Weller

Client: Industrial Supply Company

Purpose or Occasion: Race Series

Number of Colors: 4

Design Firm: SullivanPerkins

All Design: Art Garcia

Client: Topanga Plaza

Purpose or Occasion: Promotion of food court opening

Number of Colors: 5

Design Firm: Sackett Design
Art Director: Mark Sackett
Designers: Mark Sackett,
Wayne Sakamoto
Type: Mark Sackett, Wayne Sakamoto
Client: Marin Ballet
Purpose or Occasion: Fund-raiser
Number of Colors: 5

Students and dancers sold these T-shirts to raise
money for the Marin Ballet School.

◄

Design firm: Supon Design Group, Inc.
Art Directors: Supon Phornirunlit,
Jacque Coughlin
Designer: Steven Morris
Illustrator: Steven Morris
Client: Wolf Trap
Purpose or Occasion: Merchandising
Number of Colors: 4

▶

Design Firm: JOED Design Inc.
Art Director: Edward Rebek
Designers: Edward Rebek,
Joanne Rebek
Client: JOED Design Inc.
Purpose or Occasion: Holiday
promotion
Number of Colors: 3
Imagine the Possibilities T-shirt was mailed in
a blue tube with metallic stars and gold foil.

Design Firm: Ascent Communications

Art Director: Al Haeger

Designer: Al Haeger

Illustrator: Darrel Tank

Client: Spectrum Naturals, Inc.

Purpose or Occasion: Promotion

Number of Colors: 8

A reproduction of Spectrum Naturals' organic olive oil label was printed on a 100% organically grown cotton T-shirt.

Design Firm: Gil Shuler Graphic Design, Inc.
All Design: Gil Shuler
Client: The Dart Club
Purpose or Occasion: Party promotion
Number of Colors: 3

© 1993 JOHN EVANS

▲

Design Firm: John Evans Design
All Design: John Evans
Purpose or Occasion: Retail
Number of Colors: 1

◄

Design Firm: Pentagram Design
Art Director: Paula Scher
Designers: Paula Scher, Ron Louie, Lisa Mazur
Client: American Museum of Natural History
Purpose or Occasion: Retail
Number of Colors: 1
The T-shirt's dinosaur skeleton is part of the American Museum of Natural History's visual identity, used on promotional materials from banners to caps and coffee mugs.

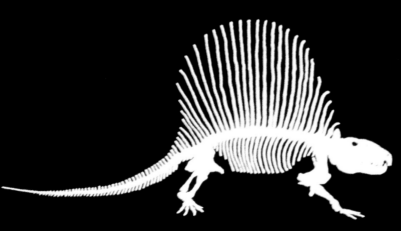

American Museum of Natural History

Designer: Sam Samanich

Illustrator: Sam Samanich

Client: UTE-T

Purpose or Occasion: Tourism

Number of Colors: 7

Design Firm: John Evans Design
All Design: John Evans
Purpose or Occasion: Retail
Number of Colors: 5

Design Firm: Lee Reedy Design Associates
All Design: Lee Reedy
Client: American Water Works Association
Purpose or Occasion: Annual conference in San Antonio, Texas
Number of Colors: 3

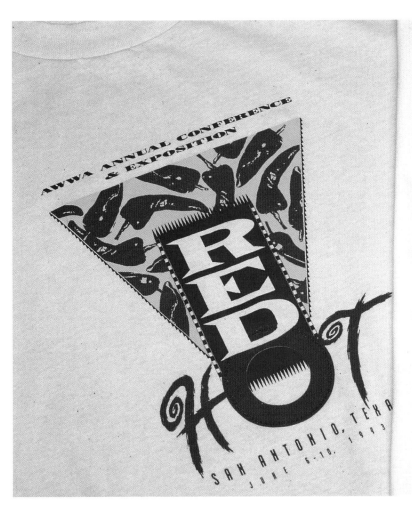

▲

Design Firm: Baldino Design
All Design: Patt Baldino
Client: Playtex
Purpose or Occasion: Promotion
Number of Colors: 3

T-shirts were created as promotional pieces for sales meetings which took place in Acapulco.

▶

Design Firm: Lehner & Whyte
Art Directors: Donna Lehner, Hugh Whyte
Designers: Hugh Whyte, Donna Lehner
Illustrator: Hugh Whyte
Client: FX4U
Purpose or Occasion: Retail
Number of Colors: 3

◄

Design Firm: John Evans Design
All Design: John Evans
Purpose or Occasion: Retail
Number of Colors: 3

▶

Design Firm: Gibbs Baronet
Art Directors: Steve Gibbs, Willie Baronet
Designers: Meta Newhouse, Steve Gibbs
Client: Kimberly-Clark
Purpose or Occasion: Given to recipients of Kimberly-Clark's scholarships.
Number of Colors: 3

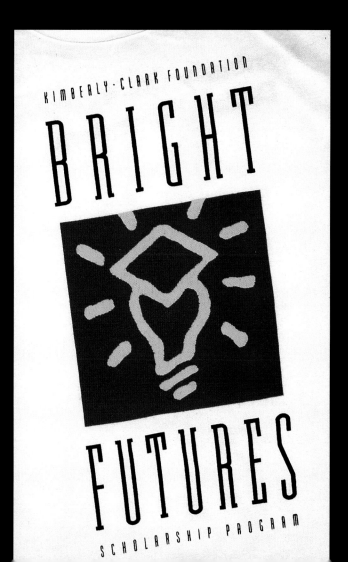

Design Firm: Hi-Flow Graphics
All Design: Susanna Guizar
Client: Los Angeles Search Dogs
Purpose or Occasion: Fund-raiser
& retail
Number of Colors: 4

Design Firm: Heartland Apparel
Art Director: Kathy Berwald
Designer: Johnny Wilson
Illustrator: Johnny Wilson
Client: MGM
Number of Colors: 5

Design Firm: Art Guy Studios
All Design: James F. Kraus
Client: Art Guy Studios
Purpose or Occasion: Give-away for clients
Number of Colors: 2

Design Firm: Cloud and Gehshan Associates, Inc.
Art Director: Jerome Cloud
Designers: Jerome Cloud, Dorothy Funderwhite
Illustrator: Kent Massey
Client: City of Philadelphia
Purpose or Occasion: Identity for new downtown bus loop
Number of Colors: 5

Design Firm: Golden Squeegee Productions

All Design: Jim Popp

Client: Dog & Pony Days

Purpose or Occasion: Dog & Pony
Product Line

Number of Colors: 11

This colorful, classic, yet non-traditional T-shirt
design promotes the *Dog & Pony* product line
with a new western flavor.

Design Firm: Rickabaugh Graphics
All Design: Eric Rickabaugh
Client: The Art Director's Club of Cincinnati
Purpose or Occasion: Give-away
Number of Colors: 3
These shirts were created as a give-away item at a presentation by Eric Rickabaugh to the Art Directors Club of Cincinnati.

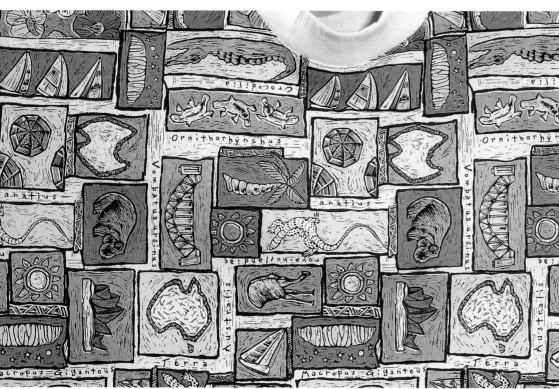

Design Firm: Textile Printers Pty. Ltd.
Art Director: George Raimondo
Designer: George Raimondo
Illustrator: Julie Lynch
Client: Goanna Gear Australia
Purpose or Occasion: Retail
Number of Colors: 5

◄

Design Firm: Supon Design Group, Inc.
Art Directors: Supon Phornirunlit, Andrew Dolan
Designer: Andrew Dolan
Illustrator: Andrew Dolan
Client: Planet Called Earth
Purpose or Occasion: Retail
Number of Colors: 4

Design Firm: Mirror Image, Inc.

All Design: Jose Ortega

Client: Amnesty International

Purpose or Occasion: Human rights awareness

Number of Colors: 5

Design Firm: Jon Flaming Design
All Design: Jon Flaming
Client: The Dallas Zoo
Purpose or Occasion: 10K run
Number of Colors: 2

Design Firm: Intense Tee's
Art Directors: John J. Mazur III,
Jim Bombolevicz
Designer: John J. Mazur III
Client: Intense Tee's
Purpose or Occasion: Retail
Number of Colors: 2

Design Firm: Cyber Graphics
All Design: Jean Busky
Client: Johnson Bryce Corp.
Purpose or Occasion: Annual picnic
Number of Colors: 3

▶

Design Firm: Lee Reedy Design Associates
All Design: Lee Reedy
Client: MCI
Purpose or Occasion: Introduction
of MCI's direct-sales division
Number of Colors: 4

Design Firm: Sommese Design

All Design: Lanny Sommese

Client: Central Pennsylvania Festival of the Arts

Purpose or Occasion: Retail

Number of Colors: 4

The Central Pennsylvania Festival of the Arts commissioned this T-shirt for their annual summer festival of visual and performing arts.

THE AMERICAS

ATHLETIC CLUB

DALLAS

Design Firm: John Evans Design
All Design: John Evans
Client: The Americas Athletic Club

▶

Design Firm: Mires Design, Inc.
All Design: John Ball
Client: Mires Design, Inc.
Purpose or Occasion: Give-away
to clients and vendors
Number of Colors: 2

◀

Design Firm: Boston College Office of Communications
All Design: Karen E. Roehr
Client: Boston College Liturgical Dance Ensemble
Purpose or Occasion: Annual Christmas Dance
Performance
Number of Colors: 2

The T-shirt was designed to celebrate an annual Liturgical
Christmas Dance, *A Dancer's Christmas*, referred to as a
religious version of *The Nutcracker*.

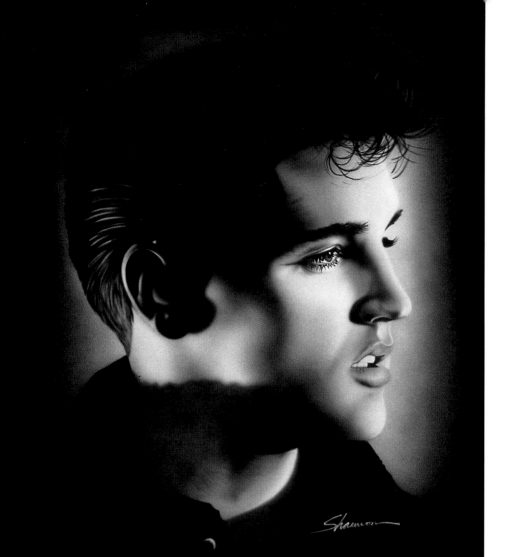

◀

Design Firm: Shannon Gallery
All Design: Shannon
Purpose or Occasion: Retail
Number of Colors: 1

▶

Design Firm: Dyer/Mutchnick Group
Art Director: Rod Dyer
Designer: Oris Yamashita
Client: All-Girl Productions
Purpose or Occasion: Concert tour T-shirt for Bette Midler
Number of Colors: 4

Design Firm: Shannon Gallery
All Design: Shannon
Purpose or Occasion: Retail
Number of Colors: 10

TEXAS

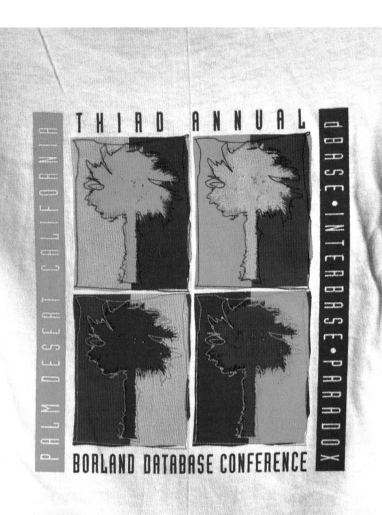

Design Firm: 90° Angle
All Design: Kim Sager
Client: 90° Angle
Purpose or Occasion: Retail
Number of Colors: 5
This design is reminiscent of a popular 1960s
T-shirt that read, "War is unhealthy...for children
and other living things."

Design Firm: Sommese Design

All Design: Kristin Sommese

Client: PSU's Beta Sigma Beta

Purpose or Occasion: Regatta to benefit the American Cancer Society

Number of Colors: 3

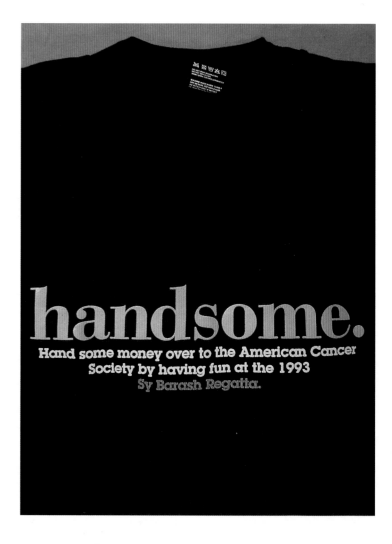

Design Firm: 90° Angle

All Design: Kim Sager

Client: 90° Angle

Purpose or Occasion: New design for show

Number of Colors: 3

HEALTHY

TRUTH

BEAUTY

THINK

HAPPY

Design Firm: PandaMonium Designs
Art Director: Raymond Yu
Designers: Raymond Yu, Daniel Yee
Illustrator: Daniel Yee
Client: Goal Line Sports Equipment
Purpose or Occasion: Promotion
Number of Colors: 4

◀

Design Firm: A.C. Designs
Designer: Anne H. Cronier
Client: Mountain State Wheelers Bicycle Club
Purpose or Occasion: Bicycle Club Ride
Number of Colors: 3

▶

Design Firm: Alphawave Designs
All Design: Douglas Dunbebin
Client: Alphawave/National Organization
for Women
Purpose or Occasion: Fund-raiser
Number of Colors: 4

Design Firm: Sayles Graphic Design
All Design: John Sayles
Client: Sayles Graphic Design
Purpose or Occasion: Gift
Number of Colors: 3

Part of a series of shirts given to clients and suppliers, this T-shirt uses "Tip Top Design" as its theme.

Design Firm: Sayles Graphic Design
All Design: John Sayles

Design Firm: Art Guy Studios
All Design: James F. Kraus
Client: WZBC 90.3 FM
Purpose or Occasion: Benefit premium
Number of Colors: 1

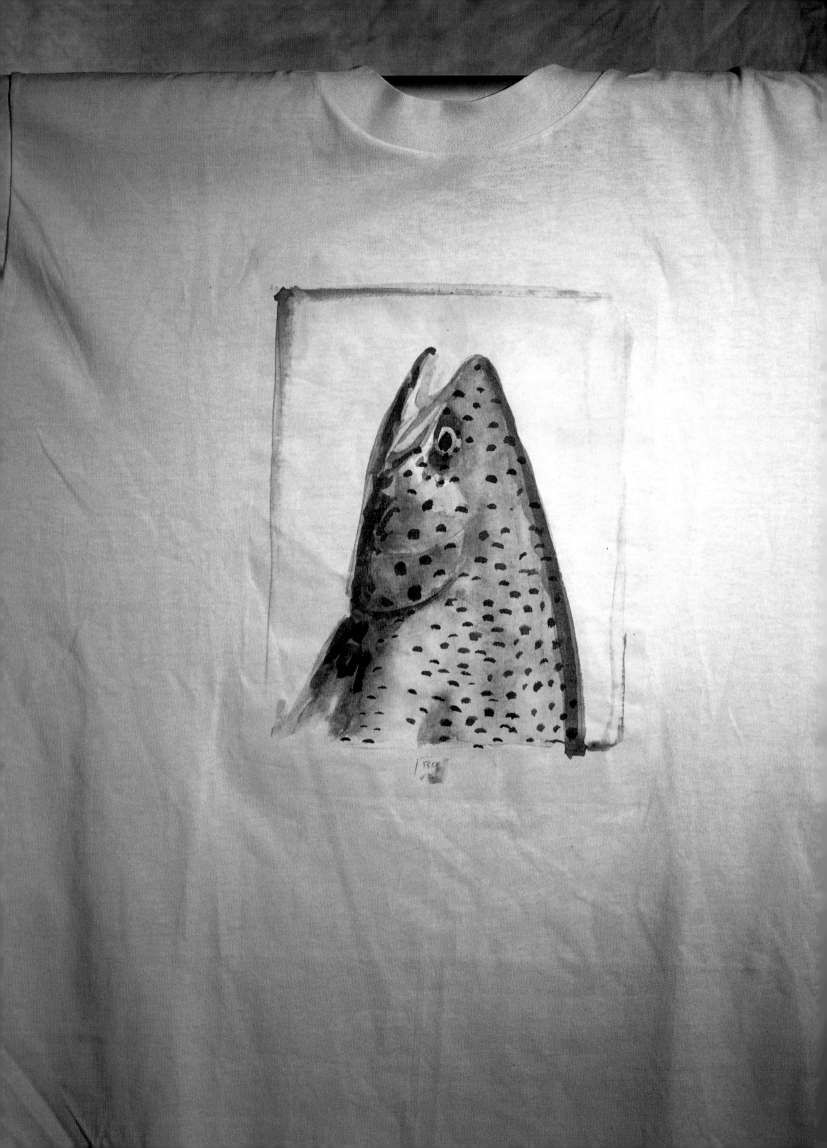

Design Firm: Garrabrandt Enterprises, Inc.
All Design: Bruce S. Garrabrandt
Purpose or Occasion: Retail
Number of Colors: 5
An original colored pencil drawing painted on a T-shirt depicts the artist's theory that cows are notoriously bad drivers.

CATTLE

DRIVE

ANTARCTIC

DOMINOES

Design Firm: Dean Johnson Design
All Design: Bruce Dean
Client: Dean Johnson Design
Purpose or Occasion: Self-promotion & retail
Number of Colors: 4

Design Firm: Garrabrandt Enterprises, Inc.
All Design: Bruce S. Garrabrandt
Purpose or Occasion: Retail
Number of Colors: 5
This original colored pencil drawing painted on a T-shirt proposes that penguins are proof that God has a sense of humor.

Design Firm: Ricardo Beron Castro
All Design: Ricardo Beron Castro
Purpose or Occasion: Retail
Number of Colors: 5

▶

◀

Design Firm: 90° Angle
All Design: Kim Sager
Client: Prelude Design
Purpose or Occasion: Summer retail
Number of Colors: 5
This T-shirt is designed to bring attention to pollution problems.

▶

Design Firm: Williams & Co.
Art Director: Iris Williams
Designer: Charles Williams
Illustrator: Charles Williams
Client: Williams & Co.
Purpose or Occasion: Personal
artistic expression

Design Firm: Dyer/Mutchnick Group, Inc.
All Design: Rod Dyer
Client: Pane e Vino Trattoria
Purpose or Occasion: Promotion
Number of Colors: 3

BIG JOE

▲

Design Firm: 90° Angle
All Design: Kim Sager
Client: 90° Angle
Purpose or Occasion: Retail

◄

Design Firm: Ken Brown Designs
Designer: Ken Brown
Purpose or Occasion: Retail
Number of Colors: 5

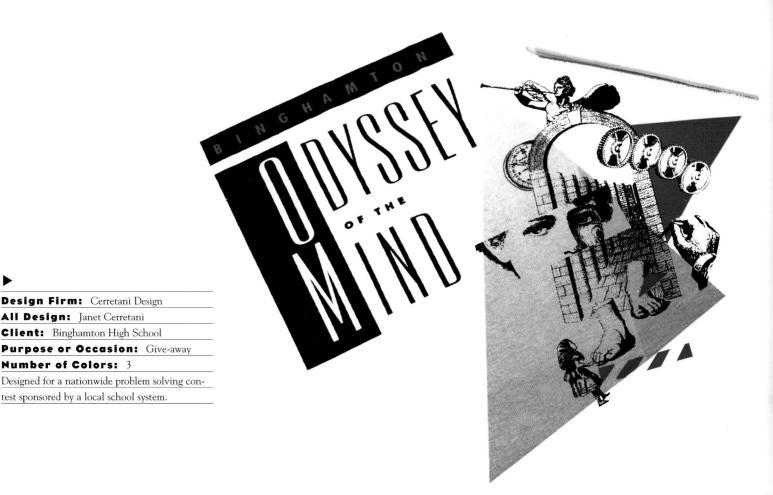

Design Firm: Cerretani Design
All Design: Janet Cerretani
Client: Binghamton High School
Purpose or Occasion: Give-away
Number of Colors: 3
Designed for a nationwide problem solving contest sponsored by a local school system.

Design Firm: Cerretani Design
All Design: Janet Cerretani
Client: Rocky Mountain Helicopters
Purpose or Occasion: Give-away
Number of Colors: 4
The shirt was a gift to helicopter operators for the end-of-the-season logging push in Alaska.

Purpose or Occasion: In-house retail

Number of Colors: 4

The design was created for sale to employees and
members of the hospital staff to help raise money
for the hospital.

▲

Design Firm: Sayles Graphic Design
All Design: John Sayles
Client: Sayles Graphic Design
Purpose or Occasion: Gift to clients and suppliers
Number of Colors: 3

▼

Design Firm: Russell Leong Design
All Design: Russell K. Leong
Client: Digidesign
Purpose or Occasion: Promotion
Number of Colors: 2

▶

Design Firm: Russell Leong Design
All Design: Russell K. Leong
Client: City of Palo Alto
Purpose or Occasion: Black & White Ball
Number of Colors: 2

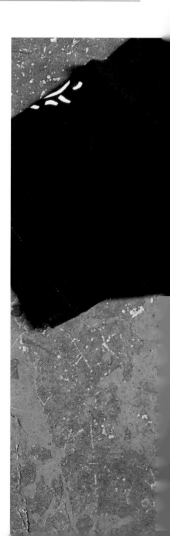

◀

All Design: Bink
Client: Dudaman Active Wear
Purpose or Occasion: Retail
Number of Colors: 1

Design Firm: John Evans Design

All Design: John Evans

Client: Sol's Taco Lounge & Tango Bar

Purpose or Occasion: Employee uniform

Number of Colors: 1

◀

Design Firm: Gibbs Baronet

Art Director: Steve Gibbs, Willie Baronet

Designer: Jonathan Ingram

Illustrator: Jonathan Ingram

Client: Walter Ego

Purpose or Occasion: Introduction of a new line of T-shirts

Number of Colors: 1

▶

Design Firm: Signature Screencraft Ltd.

All Design: John Trewin

Client: Yaga McInnes

Purpose or Occasion: Fund-raiser

Number of Colors: 5

This T-shirt was designed using a mosaic technique: the shirt's concept employs ethnic heritage to promote the fund-raising activities of a local, Italian dance group.

Design Firm: SullivanPerkins
Art Director: Ron Sullivan
Designer: Kelly Allen
Illustrator: Kelly Allen
Client: Mental Health Association
Purpose or Occasion: Promotion of Mental Health Association of Dallas
Number of Colors: 3

MENTAL HEALTH

THINK ABOUT IT IN A

WHOLE NEW LIGHT

MENTAL HEALTH ASSOCIATION OF GREATER DALLAS

Design Firm: Sommese Design
Art Director: Kristin Sommese
Designer: Audrey Rosenberg
Illustrator: Audrey Rosenberg
Client: PSU IFC/Panhellenic Council
Purpose or Occasion: Dance-marathon benefit for children with cancer
Number of Colors: 4

GROWING STRONGER TOGETHER

PSU IFC PANHELLENIC 94
DANCE MARATHON

◀

Design Firm: Sayles Graphic Design
All Design: John Sayles
Client: American Institute of Architects
Purpose or Occasion: Promotion & commemoration
Number of Colors: 4

Designed to coordinate with a poster for the event, this T-shirt features a sandcastle character.

▼

Design Firm: Fountainhead Advertising
All Design: Dory Colbert
Copywriter: Dory Colbert
Client: Grant Elementary School
Purpose or Occasion: Word of the Year
Number of Colors: 3

Another version of the fund-raiser T-shirt. "Attitude" was the school's "word of the year," and the shirt emphasizes a positive, "I can do it" attitude. Design work was donated by the designer-who is a parent of a Grant student.

▲

Design Firm: Mike Salisbury
Communications
Art Director: Mike Salisbury
Designer: Patrick O'Neal
Illustrator: Patrick O'Neal
Client: GOTCHA
Purpose or Occasion: Retail
Number of Colors: 7

▲

Design Firm: Mike Salisbury
Communications
All Design: Mike Salisbury
Client: GOTCHA
Purpose or Occasion: Retail
Number of Colors: 5

▶

All Design: Mary M. Sheetz
Client: UTE-T's
Purpose or Occasion: Reprint line
Number of Colors: 6

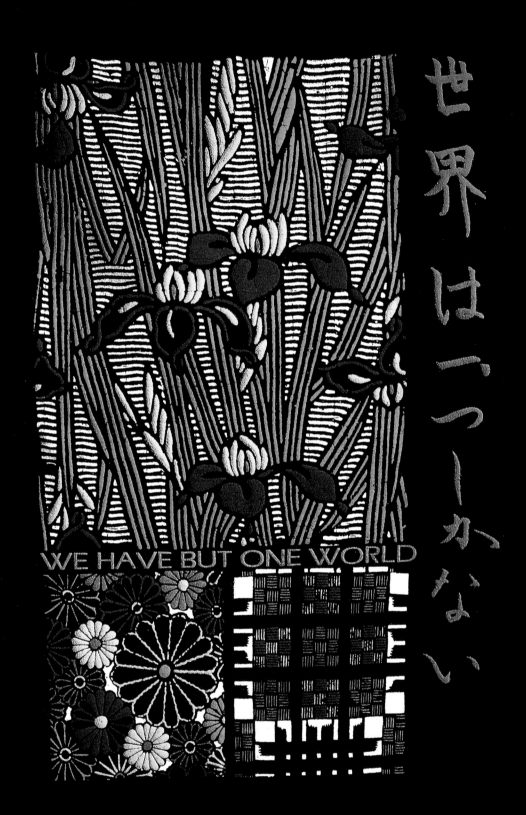

WE HAVE BUT ONE WORLD

世界は一つーかない

▲

Design Firm: Animus Communicacao
Art Director: Rique Nitzsche
Designer: Felicio Torres
Photographer: Guido Paterno
Client: Texaco Brasil
Purpose or Occasion: Sailing regatta
Number of Colors: 2

Design Firm: Eureka Advertising
Art Director: Javier Arcos Pitarque
Designer: Javier Arcos Pitarque
Illustrator: Angel Camino
Client: Eureka Advertising
Purpose or Occasion: Second anniversary celebration
Number of Colors: 4

DIRECTORY

90° Angle
120 East 36th Street
New York, NY 10016

A.C. Designs
P.O. Box 6633
Charleston, WV 85362

Aardvark Graphics
3149 Grand Avenue South
Minneapolis, MN 55408

Alphawave Designs
3557 Cherry Hill Court
Beltsville, MD 20705

Animus Communicacao
Ladeira Do Ascurra 115-A
222 41-320, Rio
Brazil

Applegate Art & Design
1606-30 Street
Des Moines, IA 50310

Art Guy Studios
195 W. Canton Street
Boston, MA 02116

Ascent Communications
64 Deep Creek Bench
Livingston, MT 59047

Baldino Design
64 Vernon Drive
Scarsdale, NY 10583

Barb-Wire Designs
10211 Swanton Drive
Santee, CA 92071

Ricardo Beron Castro
Cr. 10 #93A-48 Apto. 303
Staffe de Bogota
Colombia

Blue Chicago
State & Chestnut
Chicago, IL 60602

The Bon Marche
Third & Pine Street
Seattle, WA 98181

Boston College Office
of Communications
K. E. Roehr
230 Babcock Street 3A
Brookline, MA 012146

Ken Brown Designs
Mirror Image, Inc.
251 Albany Street
Cambridge, MA 02139

Bullet Communications, Inc.
200 S. Midland Avenue
Joliet, IL 60436

CTM Manufacturing
(Bi Bi Dee)
4773 58th Avenue N
St. Petersberg, FL 33714

Callahan & Co.
Advertising
9 West 29th Street
Baltimore, MD 21218

Cerretani Design
2224C Pierce Creek Road
Binghamton, NY 13903

Charney Design
1120 Whitewater Cove
Santa Cruz, CA 95062

Cloud and Gehshan
Associates, Inc.
622 South 10th Street
Philadelphia, PA 19147

Crabtree & Scrussion Design
1712 Graham Road
Reynoldsburg, OH 43068

Creative Pig Minds
105 Hall Street
Rockford, IL 61107

Cyber Graphics
3825 Delp Street
Memphis, TN 38118

C. Benjamin Dacus
3106 Moss Side Avenue
Richmond, VA 23222

The Design Company
One Baltimore Place
Suite A-850
Atlanta, GA 30308

Dyer/Mutchnick Group, Inc.
8360 Melrose Avenue
3rd Floor
Los Angeles, CA 90069

Elton Ward Design
P.O. Box 802
Parramatta NWS 2124
Australia

Entheos Design
11121 63rd Avenue
Kenosha, WI 53142

Eureka Advertising
Serrano 41 60-13
Madrid
Spain

John Evans Design
2200 North Lamar
Suite 220
Dallas, TX 75202

Barbara Ferguson Designs
10211 Swanton Drive
Santee, CA 92071

Fotofolio/Mirror Image, Inc.
251 Albany Street
Cambridge, MA 02139

Fountainhead Advertising
P.O. Box 993
Columbia, MO 65205

Garrabrandt Enterprises, Inc.
1505 Newport Drive]
Lakewood, NJ 08701

Gibbs Baronet
2200 N. Lamar, #201
Dallas, TX 75202

Sandy Gin
335 High Street
Palo Alto, CA 94301

Golden Squeegee
Productions
900 Santa Fe Drive
Denver, CO 80204

Heartland Apparel
3149 Grand Avenue South
Minneapolis, MN 55408

Hi-Flow Graphics
14512 Filmore Street
Arleta, CA 91331

High Cotton, Inc.
9 Commerce Place
Bluffton, SC 29910
Joan C. Hollingsworth
2824 NE 22 Avenue
Portland, OR

Hon Blue Inc.
501 Summer Street #3B1
Honolulu, HI 96817

Intense Tee's
P.O. Box 128
121 Hawkins Place
Boonton, NJ 07005

JQED Design Inc.
559 Spring Road
Elmhurst, IL 60126

Johnson Graphics
20 Salem Street
Newburyport, MA 01950

Dean Johnson Design
604 Fort Wayne Avenue
Indianapolis, IN 46204

Jon Flaming Design
2200 North Lamar
Dallas, TX 75202

Joss Design Group
One East Erie
Suite 310
Chicago, IL 60611

A. Kaligos & Co.
Industrial Area of Thermi
57001 Thermi
Greece

Kenzo
STABATEX,
M. Simos & Co.
49 Lefkas Street
Patras 263 33
Greece

Michael Kern Design
449 Santa Fe Drive #177
Encinitas, CA 92024

Karyl Klopp Design
5209 8th Street
Charlestown, MA 02129

Lania Ink, Inc.
P.O. Box 3948
Agana 96910
Guam

Lehner & Whyte
8-10 South Fullerton Avenue
Montclair, NJ 07042

Russell Leong Design
847 Emerson Street
Palo Alto, CA 94301

McCargar Design
3906 Silverado Trail
Calistoga, CA 94515

MC Studio/Times
Mirror Magazines
2 Park Avenue
New York, NY 10016

Mires Design, Inc.
2345 Kettner Blvd.
San Diego, CA 92101

Mirror Image, Inc.
251 Albany Street
Cambridge, MA 02139

Marlene Montgomery
Design
5720 W. Huron
Chicago, IL 60644

Morla Design
463 Bryant Street
San Francisco, CA 94107

Ogre's Alley
510 Decatur Street
Hoffman Estates, IL 60194

PandaMonium Designs
14 Mt. Hood Road
Suite 3
Boston, MA 02135

Alex Paradowski Graphic
Design
424 South Clay
St. Louis, MO 63122

Pentagram Design
212 Fifth Avenue
New York, NY 10010

Pictogram Studio
1740 U Street NW #2
Washington, DC 20009

Propaganda Screenprinting
2222 W. Belmont
Chicago, IL 60618
Joseph Rattan Design
4445 Travis #104
Dallas, TX 75205

Lee Reedy Design Associates
1542 Williams Street
Denver, CO 80218

Reliv, Inc.
136 Chesterfield Industrial
Blvd.
Chesterfield, MO 63005

Richards and Swensen, Inc.
350 South 400 East
Suite 300
Salt Lake City, UT 84111

Rickabaugh Graphics
384 W. Johnstown Road
Cahanna, OH 43230

The Riordon Design
Group, Inc.
1001 Queen Street West
Mississauga, Ontario L5H
4E1
Canada

RIP Ink.
814 Brandon Avenue
Norfolk, VA 23517

K. E. Roehr
Design/Illustration
230 Babcock Street 3A
Brookline, MA 02146

Sackett Design
2103 Scott Street
San Francisco, CA 94115

Mike Salisbury
Communications
2200 Amapola Court
Suite 202
Torrance, CA 90501

Sayles Graphic Design
308 Eighth Street
Des Moines, IA 50309

Gil Schuler Graphic
Design, Inc.
231 King Street
Charleston, SC 29401

Scoville Creative
631 West Wellington
Chicago, IL 60657

Segura, Inc.
361 W. Chestnut 1st Floor
Chicago, IL 60610

Clifford Selbert Design
2067 Massachusetts Avenue
Cambridge, MA 02140

Shannon Gallery
29 Station Road
Bayville, NJ 08721

Sibley Peteet Design
965 Slucom
Dallas, TX 75207

Signature Screencraft Ltd.
165 Colonnade Road
Neprau Ontario K2E 7J4
Canada

Sommese Design
481 Glenn Road
State College, PA 16803

Speak, Inc.
1476 W. Grace Street
Chicago, IL 60613

Spirit River Design
1250 72nd Avenue NE #203
Fridley, MN 55432

Sportdecals
365 East Terra Cotta Avenue
Crystal Lake, IL 60014

SullivanPerkins
2811 McKinney, Suite 320,
LB 111
Dallas, TX 75204

Supon Design Group, Inc.
1700 K Street, NW, Ste. 400
Washington, DC 20006

Tayco Screen Printing
25 W. Las Vegas
Colorado Springs, CO 80903

Textile Printers Pty. Ltd.
124 Tolley Road
St. Agnes 5097
S. Australia
Lee Tyin
56 Livingston Street 2C
Brooklyn, NY 11201

Walcott-Ayers Group
1230 Preservation Park
Oakland, CA 94612

The Weller Institute for the
Cure of Design
P.O. Box 518
1575 W. Highway 32
Oakley, UT 84055

Williams & Co.
21 R. Railroad Avenue
Rockport, MA 01966

X-Design Co.
1606 30th Street
Des Moines, IA 50310

ZEDWEAR
1718 M Street, NW
Suite 101
Washington, DC 20036